QUOTES FROM THE GREATEST ENTREPRENEURS

★ ★ ★

STEVE JOBS

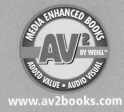

www.av2books.com

AV² provides enriched content that supplements and complements this book. Weigl's AV² books strive to create inspired learning and engage young minds in a total learning experience.

Your AV² Media Enhanced books come alive with...

Audio
Listen to sections of the book read aloud.

Key Words
Study vocabulary, and complete a matching word activity.

Go to **www.av2books.com**, and enter this book's unique code.

Video
Watch informative video clips.

Quizzes
Test your knowledge.

BOOK CODE

U 7 7 9 3 7 9

Embedded Weblinks
Gain additional information for research.

Slide Show
View images and captions, and prepare a presentation.

AV² by Weigl brings you media enhanced books that support active learning.

Try This!
Complete activities and hands-on experiments.

... and much, much more!

Published by AV² by Weigl
350 5th Avenue, 59th Floor
New York, NY 10118
Websites: www.av2books.com   www.weigl.com

Library of Congress Control Number: 2015930409

ISBN 978-1-4896-3356-9 (hardcover)
ISBN 978-1-4896-3357-6 (softcover)
ISBN 978-1-4896-3358-3 (single user eBook)
ISBN 978-1-4896-3359-0 (multi-user eBook)

Printed in the United States of America in Brainerd, Minnesota
1 2 3 4 5 6 7 8 9 0 19 18 17 16 15

032015
WEP022615

Project Coordinator: Katie Gillespie   Art Director: Terry Paulhus

Every reasonable effort has been made to trace ownership and to obtain permission to reprint copyright material. The publishers would be pleased to have any errors or omissions brought to their attention so that they may be corrected in subsequent printings.

Weigl acknowledges Getty Images, iStock, and Corbis as its primary image suppliers for this title.

CONTENTS

STEVE JOBS

As a young man, Steve Jobs faced his fair share of challenges. He had difficulty in school and even dropped out of college. However, despite these obstacles, Jobs is remembered by many as one of the world's most noteworthy **entrepreneurs**.

As an adult, Jobs worked hard to reach his full potential. Along with Steve Wozniak and Ronald Wayne, he created Apple Computer, Inc. on April 1, 1976. Now called Apple Inc., the company offers some of the most popular products in the world. With innovative technology such as the **iPhone** and the **iPad**, Apple has become an extremely successful brand.

The Apple II was Apple Computer, Inc.'s first computer with a color display.

Since his passing on October 5, 2011, Jobs has left behind an incredible **legacy**. His story is proof that talent, determination, and perseverance can lead to success. The inspiring words of Steve Jobs provide both motivation and encouragement for those who aim to achieve greatness.

Steve Jobs sold his vehicle to help raise funds to start Apple Computer, Inc.

"Everything around you that you call life was made up by people that were no smarter than you. **And you can change it, you can influence it, you can build your own things that other people can use.**"

"That's been one of my mantras—focus and simplicity. **Simple can be harder than complex.** You have to work hard to get your **thinking clean to make it simple.**"

"Innovation distinguishes between a **leader and a follower**."

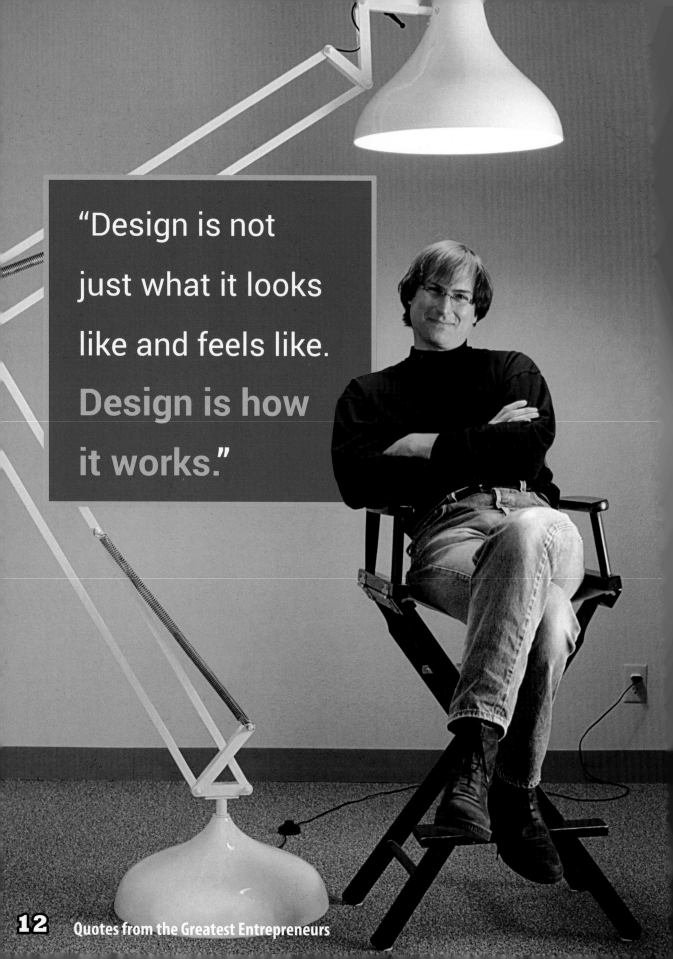

"Design is not just what it looks like and feels like. Design is how it works."

Quotes from the Greatest Entrepreneurs

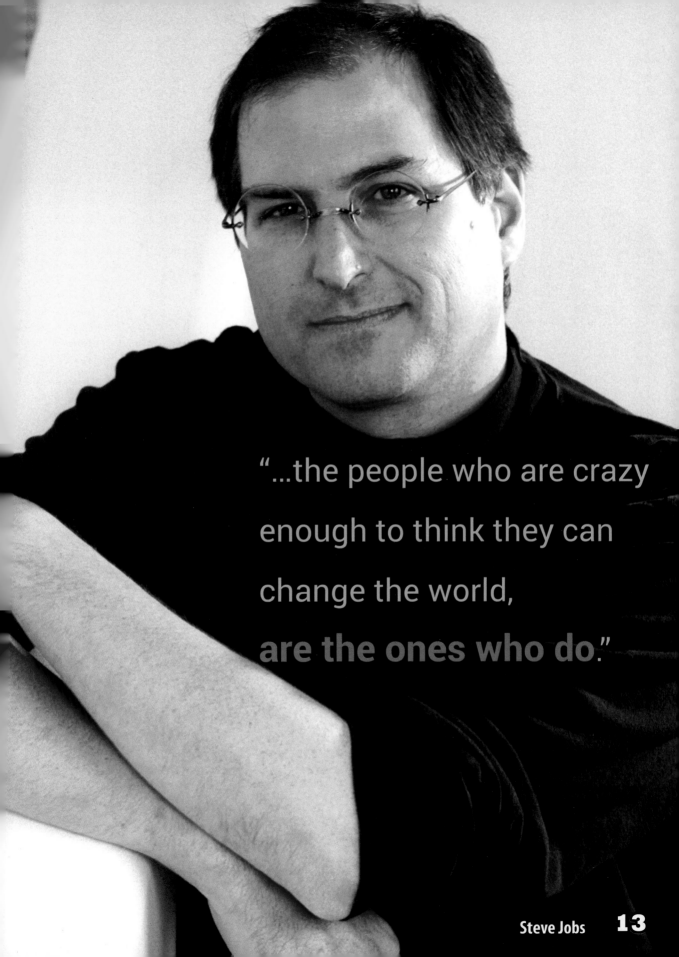

"...the people who are crazy enough to think they can change the world, **are the ones who do.**"

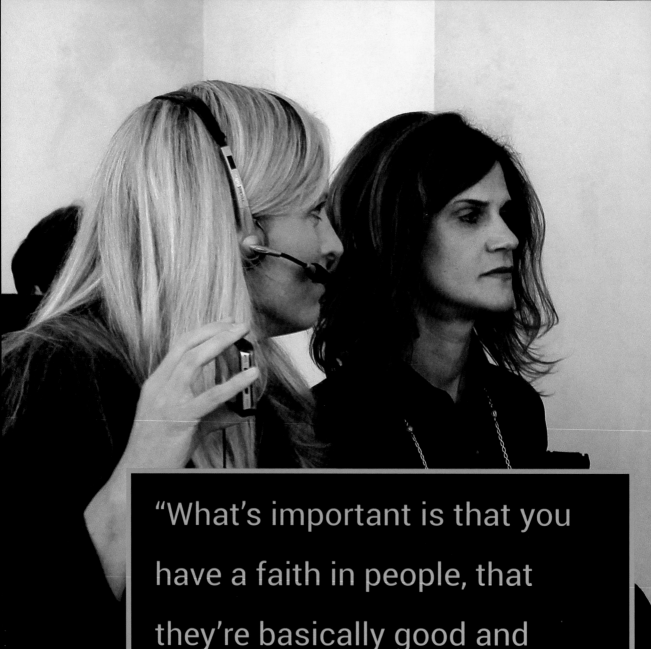

"What's important is that you have a faith in people, that they're basically good and smart, **and if you give them tools, they'll do wonderful things with them.**"

"**I'm convinced** that about half of **what separates** the successful entrepreneurs from the non-successful ones **is pure perseverance.**"

"The only way to
do great work is to
love what you do."

WRITE A BIOGRAPHY

Life Story

A person's life story can be the subject of a book. This kind of book is called a **biography**. Biographies often describe the lives of people who have achieved great success. These people may be alive today, or they may have lived many years ago. Reading a biography can help you learn more about a great person.

Steve Jobs
1955-2011

Help and Obstacles
- Did this individual have a positive attitude?
- Did this person have a **mentor**?
- Did this person face any hardships?
- If so, how were the hardships overcome?

Biography Brainstorming

Childhood
- Where and when was this person born?
- Describe his or her parents, siblings, and friends.
- Did this person grow up in unusual circumstances?

Success in the Workforce
- What records does this person hold?
- What has he or she achieved?
- How does he or she measure professional success?

Get the Facts

Use this book, and research in the library and on the internet, to find out more about your favorite entrepreneur. Learn as much about this person as you can. Where did his or her first big idea come from? What are his or her strategies for success? Has he or she set any records? Also, be sure to write down key events in the person's life. What was his or her childhood like? What has he or she accomplished? Is there anything else that makes this person special or unusual?

Accomplishments
- What is this person's life's work?
- Has he or she received awards or recognition for accomplishments?
- How have this person's accomplishments served others?

Your Opinion
- What did you learn from the books you read in your research?
- Would you suggest these books to others?
- Was anything missing from these books?

Creating a Biography

Brainstorming can be a useful research tool. Read the questions listed in each category. Answer these questions in your notebook. Your answers will help you write a biography.

Work and Preparation
- What was this person's education?
- What was his or her work experience?
- How does this person work? What is the process he or she uses?

Adulthood
- Does he or she have a family?
- What roles have prepared him or her for a career as an entrepreneur?
- How have his or her relationships influenced his or her success?

BY THE NUMBERS

Many **milestones** mark the path of a successful entrepreneur. Each achievement offers a glimpse into the life and career of Steve Jobs. Consider these fascinating facts to gain a better understanding of the man behind the quotes.

More than 300
The number of Apple Stores worldwide.

4,583
The number of **iPhones** sold every hour.

$666.66
The amount **Apple's first** computer sold for in 1976.

The year Steve Jobs met Steve Wozniak, co-founder of Apple Computer, Inc.
1969

$1
The **annual salary** Steve Jobs had at Apple Inc.

30,000
The number of people employed at American Apple Stores.

KEY WORDS

biography: an account of a person's life, written by another person

entrepreneurs: people who start a business and assume any potential risks associated with it

iPad: a handheld tablet computing device with a touchscreen interface

iPhone: a smartphone device that includes a digital camera, a cellular phone, and internet browsing and networking capabilities

legacy: something handed down by someone who has passed away

mentor: a trusted and experienced advisor

milestones: significant events or achievements

INDEX

Log on to www.av2books.com

AV² by Weigl brings you media enhanced books that support active learning. Go to www.av2books.com, and enter the special code found on page 2 of this book. You will gain access to enriched and enhanced content that supplements and complements this book. Content includes video, audio, weblinks, quizzes, a slide show, and activities.

AV² Online Navigation

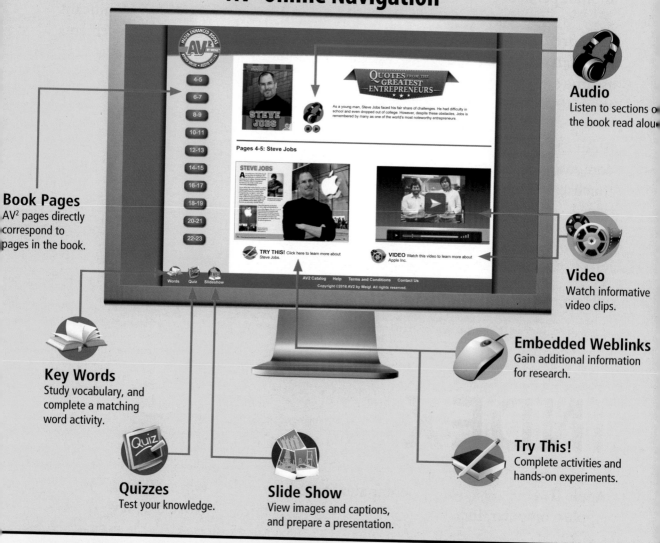

Book Pages
AV² pages directly correspond to pages in the book.

Key Words
Study vocabulary, and complete a matching word activity.

Quizzes
Test your knowledge.

Slide Show
View images and captions, and prepare a presentation.

Audio
Listen to sections o the book read alou

Video
Watch informative video clips.

Embedded Weblinks
Gain additional information for research.

Try This!
Complete activities and hands-on experiments.

AV² was built to bridge the gap between print and digital. We encourage you to tell us what you like and what you want to see in the future.

Sign up to be an AV² Ambassador at www.av2books.com/ambassador.